व्यंजन और स्वर

मार विवेक कुमार पांडे शंभूनाथ

ISBN 978-1-63873-144-3

क्रम-सूची

1

1

प्रबोध पाठ्यक्रम

PRABODH COURSE

किट

:

1

-

KIT :

1

पाठ

:

1

से

25

Lesson

-

1 to 25

अगस्त

-

किट

-

August

-

KIT

पत्राचार

पाठ्यक्रम

सधि

(हंदी)

CORRESPONDENCE COURSE WING (HINDI)

ि
ृ
द्र
ी
य
हंदी
प्रशिक्षण
संस्थान

Central Hindi Training Institute

राजभाषा
विभाग

Department of Official Language

ग

c

मंत्रालय

Ministry of Home Affairs

2
-
ए
,
प
c
थ्
ि
ी
र
ा
ज
रोड

2
-

A, Prithvi Raj Road

नई
हदल्ली
-
110011

New Delhi
-
110011

Email
-

adptracharchti

-
dol@nic.in
Phone
and
Fax No. 011
-
23017203

To download this Kit:
http://chti.rajbh
asha.gov.in/?9600?21

2

CONTENTS

IMPORTANT N
OTE
SEND YOUR RESPONSE SHEETS FOR
EVALUATION AS EARLY AS POSSIBLE
THESE ARE TAKEN INTO CONSIDERATION
FOR CALCULATING INTERNAL
ASSESSMENT MARKS.
3
FROM THE DIRECTOR'S DESK
Correspondence Course Wing (Hindi)
Central Hindi Training Institute

Department of Official Language
(Ministry of Home Affairs)
2
-
A, Prithvi Raj
Road,
New Delhi
-
110011
Dear Trainee!
You are welcome to the Prabodh Correspondence Course.
You will find herewith the First lesson
-
despatc
h. Thereafter, you will receive
subsequent lesson/units every month till March next, which will be the last despatch
before your examinations start in May. The lesson will be mailed to you in the first
week of every month.
Each despatch will be accompanied by Response
-
sheets which are to be
attempted by you and returned to us for evaluation. We attach rather greater
im
portance to your attempt on the Response
-
Sheets and in fact, it is only on the basis
of your performance in the Response
-
sheets that we are able to provide you the
proper guidance and further remedial material for improvement. Hence, I advise you to
be reg
ular in sending your Respose
-
Sheets for evaluation from the beginning itself.
Marks obtained by you in these Response
-
sheets will be counted for Internal
Assessment at the time of final examination.
I would like to stress here that since, the course of st
udy stipulated for the
Prabodh course is quite large, you
are
required to put in hard work and be regular in
studying the lessons sent to you. Our lesson despatch may, at times contain
supplementary study material also in order to complete the prescribed c
ourse in time.
Once again, I welcome you to this course and hope that our programme will
inculcate in you a new enthusiasm to learn Hindi and to use it more and more in your

official work.

Yours Sincerly,

SUMAN

LAL

Director

-

in

-

charge

4

A WORD WITH THE STUDENT

(Guidelines for Study)

Dear Student!

Through this note, we wish to let you know how we intend to plan our teaching

and in turn, how we expect you to proceed with our plan. Learni

ng a language

through correspondence is a delicate task and laxity or carelessness on your part in

keeping up plan/schedule at any stage might have an adverse effect in your progress.

Your success in making satisfactory progress will largely depend upon ho

w regular and

consistant you are in attending to our lessons and sending

us your

Response

-

Sheets,

as this will help us to keep a constant watch on your progress and to prov

ide you

regular and proper guida

nce.

WHAT WILL OUR DESPATCH CONTAIN

You will receive

our instructional material every month. Our monthly despatch will

consist

of:

(a) a kit containing lessons, (b) their response

-

sheets, and (c)

supplementary and ancillary material, whenever necessary.

(a) Lesson

Unit:

A

lesson

-

unit will contain study mate

rial for you for on

e month.

Sentence

-

patterns, vocabulary and sounds intro

duced in a particular lesson are

shown prominently at the very beginning of the lesson for your convenience. Some
of the initial lesson

-

units are concluded by a section named SUMMARY

which may

contain a tabloid gist of the lesson review material, pronunciation drill or other
practice material.

(b)

Response

-

Sheet:

Each

lesson unit will

be accompanied

by response

-

sheet

containing elaborate

d

excercise and questions to be attempted by you

. This will

enable you to actually participate in the process of learning as soon as you

finished the text

-

part of the lesson. These response

-

sheets are so designed as to

provide you practice material and at the same time, to test your attainment. These

re

sponse

-

sheets are to be attempted in your own handwriting and returned to us

for evaluation within a fortnight of its receipt.

(c) Ancillary and Supplementary

material:

A

lesson unit will be accompanied by

ancillary and supplementary material, whenever nec

essary. It may consist of charts

on consolidated material

pertaining

to various teaching points. Material for ready

reference like list of basic vocabulary, phrases and idioms, numericals, synonyms

and antonyms, charts of sentence patterns et

c.

PATTERNS OF

LESSONS

-

Each lesson will give you a graded and controlled study

material for a month. The lessons have been designed to constitute self

-

contained

2 Errors found:(Note: Please fix this to continue further)

+Looks like the book size uploaded does not match the selected size. The selected size is 8.5 in x 11 in but the uploaded size is 8 in x 11.2 in. Please reupload your book's interior in the right size. (54x on pages 1-54)

+Images/Text in the page are overlapping into the page margins. Images/Text that are beyond the page margins might be lost during printing. (1x on page 12)

1 Attention required:(Note: If this was intentional you may continue)

+We have added a blank page at the end of the book

5 Auto Fixes applied:(Note: No action is required from your side)

of 53

Zoom OutZoom In

Automatic Zoom Actual Size Page Fit Page Width 50% 75% 100% 125% 150% 200% 300% 400%

1

प्रबोध पाठ्यक्रम

PRABODH COURSE

किट

:

1

-

KIT :

1

पाठ

:

1

से

25

Lesson

-

1 to 25

अगस्त

-

किट

-

August

-

KIT

पत्राचार

पाठ्यक्रम

संधि

(

हंदी)

CORRESPONDENCE COURSE WING (HINDI)

ि

र

द्र

ी

य

हं दी

प्रशिक्षण

संस्थान

Central Hindi Training Institute

राजभाषा

विभाग

Department of Official Language

ग

ॖ

मंत्रालय

Ministry of Home Affairs

2

-

ए

,

प

ॖ

थ्

ि

ी

र

ा

ज

रोड

2

-

A, Prithvi Raj Road

नई

हदल्ली

-

110011

New Delhi

-

110011

Email

-

adptracharchti

-

dol@nic.in

Phone

and

Fax No. 011

-

23017203

To download this Kit:

http://chti.rajbh

asha.gov.in/?9600?21

2

CONTENTS

IMPORTANT N

OTE

SEND YOUR RESPONSE SHEETS FOR

EVALUATION AS EARLY AS POSSIBLE

THESE ARE TAKEN INTO CONSIDERATION

FOR CALCULATING INTERNAL

ASSESSMENT MARKS.

3

FROM THE DIRECTOR'S DESK

Correspondence Course Wing (Hindi)

Central Hindi Training Institute

Department of Official Language

(Ministry of Home Affairs)

2

-

A, Prithvi Raj
Road,
New Delhi
-
110011
Dear Trainee!
You are welcome to the Prabodh Correspondence Course.
You will find herewith the First lesson
-
despatc
h. Thereafter, you will receive
subsequent lesson/units every month till March next, which will be the last despatch
before your examinations start in May. The lesson will be mailed to you in the first
week of every month.
Each despatch will be accompanied by Response
-
sheets which are to be
attempted by you and returned to us for evaluation. We attach rather greater
im
portance to your attempt on the Response
-
Sheets and in fact, it is only on the basis
of your performance in the Response
-
sheets that we are able to provide you the
proper guidance and further remedial material for improvement. Hence, I advise you to
be reg
ular in sending your Respose
-
Sheets for evaluation from the beginning itself.
Marks obtained by you in these Response
-
sheets will be counted for Internal
Assessment at the time of final examination.
I would like to stress here that since, the course of st
udy stipulated for the
Prabodh course is quite large, you
are
required to put in hard work and be regular in
studying the lessons sent to you. Our lesson despatch may, at times contain
supplementary study material also in order to complete the prescribed c
ourse in time.
Once again, I welcome you to this course and hope that our programme will
inculcate in you a new enthusiasm to learn Hindi and to use it more and more in your
official work.
Yours Sincerly,
SUMAN
LAL

Director

-

in

-

charge

4

A WORD WITH THE STUDENT

(Guidelines for Study)

Dear Student!

Through this note, we wish to let you know how we intend to plan our teaching

and in turn, how we expect you to proceed with our plan. Learni

ng a language

through correspondence is a delicate task and laxity or carelessness on your part in

keeping up plan/schedule at any stage might have an adverse effect in your progress.

Your success in making satisfactory progress will largely depend upon ho

w regular and

consistant you are in attending to our lessons and sending

us your

Response

-

Sheets,

as this will help us to keep a constant watch on your progress and to prov

ide you

regular and proper guida

nce.

WHAT WILL OUR DESPATCH CONTAIN

You will receive

our instructional material every month. Our monthly despatch will

consist

of:

(a) a kit containing lessons, (b) their response

-

sheets, and (c)

supplementary and ancillary material, whenever necessary.

(a) Lesson

Unit:

A

lesson

-

unit will contain study mate

rial for you for on

e month.

Sentence

-

patterns, vocabulary and sounds intro

duced in a particular lesson are

shown prominently at the very beginning of the lesson for your convenience. Some

of the initial lesson

-

units are concluded by a section named SUMMARY

which may

contain a tabloid gist of the lesson review material, pronunciation drill or other

practice material.

(b)

Response

-

Sheet:

Each

lesson unit will

be accompanied

by response

-

sheet

containing elaborate

d

excercise and questions to be attempted by you

. This will

enable you to actually participate in the process of learning as soon as you

finished the text

-

part of the lesson. These response

-

sheets are so designed as to

provide you practice material and at the same time, to test your attainment. These

re

sponse

-

sheets are to be attempted in your own handwriting and returned to us

for evaluation within a fortnight of its receipt.

(c) Ancillary and Supplementary

material:

A

lesson unit will be accompanied by

ancillary and supplementary material, whenever nec

essary. It may consist of charts

on consolidated material

pertaining

to various teaching points. Material for ready

reference like list of basic vocabulary, phrases and idioms, numericals, synonyms

and antonyms, charts of sentence patterns et

c.

PATTERNS OF

LESSONS

-

Each lesson will give you a graded and controlled study

material for a month. The lessons have been designed to constitute self

–

contained